Busy Keto Cookbook

By

Ben Eugene

© 2019 Ben Eugene
Pittsburgh, PA

This publication may not be reproduced by any means in whole or in part without the prior written consent of the copyright owner.

Table of Contents

Introduction 4
Abbreviations and Equivalents 8
Entrées 10
    Deep Dish Pizza 11
    Chicken Ranch Casserole 12
    Zucchini Parmesan 13
    Amazing Chicken 14
    Turkey Chili & Cauliflower Rice 15
    Shrimp Alfredo 16
    Buffalo Chicken Meatballs 17
    Broccoli Cheddar Soup 18
    Crispy Wings – Buffalo & Garlic Parmesan 19
    Bacon Cheeseburger Soup 20
    Avocado Crab Boats 21
    Sausage Cobb Salad Lettuce Wraps 22
    Spicy Thai Coconut Chicken Soup 23
    Crab Stuffed Mushrooms with Cream Cheese 24
    Italian Hoagie Biscuits 25
    Chicken Enchilada Casserole 26
    Personal Pizza 27
    Chicken Quesadilla 28
    Chicken Peanut Pad Thai 29
    Buffalo Chicken Lettuce Wraps 30
Appetizers & Sides 31
    Zucchini French Fries 32
    Cheesy Bacon Biscuits 33

Crispy Spicy Cauliflower Pancakes 34

Cheesy Cauliflower Breadsticks 35

Sweet Onion Swiss Dip 36

Bacon Blue Cheese Deviled Eggs 37

Bacon Wrapped Jalapeno Poppers 38

Zucchini Nacho Chips 39

Mediterranean Portabella Slices 40

Sweet & Spicy Brussels Sprouts 41

Desserts 42

Peanut Butter Cookies 43

Chocolate Cheesecake 44

Minnie Blueberry Cheesecakes 45

Double Chocolate Cake 46

Chewy Ginger Cookies 48

Introduction

The Busy Keto Cookbook is written for busy people who want to eat keto. After a long day at work, school, or with the kids, it's easy to pull out a frozen dinner or order take out. Here you will find more than three weeks of keto recipes to help fit keto meals into your busy schedule. I'm confident these keto recipes will become some of your frequent favorites and help kick start a new healthy keto lifestyle.

It seems that everywhere you turn these days you see the word "keto". Ketogenic diets and keto meals are some of the most popular food trends in the world. In this introduction, you will learn a little about ketosis, ketogenic diets, and my personal experience with eating keto.

I should begin by saying that I am not a medical professional. However, you don't have to be a dietician to learn how to eat keto and be healthy. There are numerous benefits that come with eating keto such as weight loss, increased energy, and mental focus. Almost everyone can benefit from eating a low-carb, high-fat diet.

Ketosis is a natural process in the body to help us survive when food intake is low. During ketosis, we produce ketones, which are produced from the breakdown of fats in the liver. The outcome of a properly maintained keto diet is forcing your body into this metabolic state. This is not done through starvation of calories but through starvation of carbohydrates. The ketogenic diet essentially uses your body fat as an energy source which results in reduced body fat and increased weight loss.

Many people looking to increase mental performance for school or work choose to eat a ketogenic diet. Ketones are an excellent source of fuel for the brain. When you lower carb intake, you avoid big spikes in blood sugar. Together, this can result in improved focus and concentration. By giving your body a better and more reliable energy source, you will feel more energized during the day. Fats are shown to be the most effective molecule to burn as fuel. On top of that, fat is naturally more satisfying and ends up leaving us in a satisfied full state for longer.

To start a ketogenic diet, you will want to limit your carbohydrate intake. Carbohydrates should come mostly from vegetables, nuts, and dairy. You should refrain from eating any refined carbohydrates such as wheat, starch, and fruit. The small exceptions to this are avocado and berries which can be consumed in moderation.

One of the most important things to do is keep track of your daily net carb intake. I use the simplified equation for net carbs which are the total carbohydrates, minus the total fiber. Typically, you should eat anywhere between 20 – 30 grams of net carbs when starting your diet. After your body adjusts and you enter ketosis, you can reduce your daily net carb intake to 15 – 20 grams. If you are doing keto for weight loss, it's a good idea to keep track of both your total carbs and net carbs.

As you'll see in the following recipes, limiting your net carb intake is as simple as focusing on meats, cheeses, and leafy greens. Always check the nutrition facts label on food because net carbs can vary depending on the manufacturer. Some easy keto snacks include nuts, seeds, and cheeses.

My personal experience with eating keto started about a year ago. At that time I was overweight and had low energy. I found myself searching online for another diet that was probably doomed to fail like so many before them. Luckily, a friend told me about the keto diet. I thought that a diet where I could eat some of my favorite meats, cheeses, and vegetable sounded great so I gave it a try.

Since I started eating keto, I have lost a significant amount of weight. I feel more energized to tackle my day to day activities and I have also noticed better performance at work which I attribute to an increased mental performance from my ketogenic diet. However, my main goal was weight loss and I am thrilled to say that today I weigh the same today as I did when I played high school soccer.

Initially, my busy schedule made it difficult to stick to a keto diet. I had to search for recipes that were quick, easy, and delicious which wasn't an easy task after a long day at work. It was these challenges that caused me to create the Busy Keto Cookbook so that others can have success with eating keto. I hope that you enjoy this cookbook and I wish you good luck with your keto journey.

As with any diet, results may vary for each individual. Consult with your doctor or dietitian before starting something new with your nutrition, and see what works best for your body's chemistry and makeup.

Abbreviations and Equivalents

In order to make things easier for everyone across the globe, here is a list of the abbreviations I have used in the recipes and some conversions rounded to approximate equivalents.

Abbreviations

Imperial	Abbreviation
Teaspoon	tsp.
Tablespoon	tbsp.
Cup	cup
Pound	lb
Ounce (weight)	oz

Metric	Abbreviation
Milliliter	ml
Liter	L
Gram	g
Kilogram	kg

Equivalents

Imperial	Metric
1/2 tsp.	2.5 ml
1 tsp.	5 ml
1 tbsp.	15 ml
1/4 cup	60 ml

1/3 cup	80 ml
1/2 cup	120 ml
1 cup	240 ml
1 fl oz	30 ml
1 oz (weight)	28.35 g
1 lb	454 g

Entrées

Deep Dish Pizza

Total Time
45 minutes

Ingredients
2 eggs
8 oz. cream cheese
2 cups mozzarella cheese, shredded
1 lb. Italian sausage
15 oz. tomato sauce (no sugar added, unseasoned)
10 slices pepperoni
1 tbsp. oregano
1/2 tbsp. garlic powder
1/2 tbsp. red pepper flakes
Olive oil

Directions
1) Preheat oven to 350 °F.
2) Lightly coat a large round baking dish with olive oil.
3) Combine softened cream cheese, eggs, and 1/2 cup shredded mozzarella cheese. Mix well and spread evenly in baking dish. Bake for 15 minutes.
4) Cook Italian sausage in large skillet.
5) Add to tomato sauce; oregano, garlic powder, and red pepper flakes. Stir sauce until mixed.
6) Add cooked Italian sausage and sauce to the top of baked cream cheese crust.
7) Top with remaining shredded mozzarella cheese and pepperoni.
8) Bake for 15 minutes.
9) After baking, allow to sit for 5 minutes before serving.

Yield
4 servings

Chicken Ranch Casserole

Total Time
30 minutes

Ingredients
10 oz. bag steamed broccoli
1 lb. chicken breast, cooked, shredded
6 slices bacon
8 oz. sour cream
1/2 oz. ranch seasoning
1 cup colby jack cheese, shredded
1/4 cup parmesan cheese, grated

Directions
1) Preheat oven to 350 °F.
2) Lightly coat a large round baking dish with olive oil.
3) Cook bacon in a skillet. Chop cooked bacon into small strips.
4) Microwave bag steamed broccoli and drain in a colander.
5) Add ranch seasoning to sour cream and mix.
6) In a large round baking dish combine broccoli, chicken, sour cream mixture, bacon, and shredded colby jack cheese. Mix well.
7) Top with grated parmesan cheese.
8) Bake for 20 minutes.

Yield
4 servings

Zucchini Parmesan

Total Time
20 minutes

Ingredients
1 large zucchini
2 beaten eggs
1/2 cup almond flour
1 tsp. oregano
1/2 tsp. basil
3 cups tomato sauce (no sugar added, unseasoned)
1 cup parmesan cheese, grated
1 tbsp. oregano
1 tbsp. garlic powder

Directions
1) Cut zucchini into 1/2 inch slices.
2) In a small bowl, add almond flour, 1/2 cup parmesan cheese, and 1/2 tbsp. garlic powder, stir to mix.
3) Dip zucchini in beaten eggs, then dip in almond flour mixture.
4) In a skillet, place vegetable oil to a depth of 1/4 inch and heat on medium-high.
5) Sauté until golden brown, replenish vegetable oil as needed.
6) As slices brown, remove and place on paper towels.
7) Add oregano and 1/2 tbsp. garlic powder to tomato sauce and heat on medium heat.
8) Place sauce in small bowl for dipping.
9) Top zucchini with parmesan cheese.

Yield
3 servings

Amazing Chicken

Total Time
50 minutes

Ingredients
2 lbs. chicken breast
1 cup mayonnaise
1/4 cup hot sauce
2 cups parmesan cheese, grated
1 tsp. garlic powder
1 tsp. paprika
1/2 tsp. salt
1/2 tsp. pepper
Olive oil

Directions
1) Preheat oven to 350 °F.
2) Cut chicken breasts into medium sized pieces. Lightly pound chicken.
3) In a large bowl add mayonnaise and hot sauce. Stir to mix.
4) In a separate large bowl add parmesan cheese, garlic powder, paprika, salt, and pepper.
5) Dip chicken in mayonnaise mixture to coat evenly. Then dip in parmesan cheese mixture fully coating chicken breast.
6) Line baking sheet with foil and lightly coat with olive oil.
7) Evenly space chicken breasts on the baking sheet.
8) Bake for 40 minutes.

Yield
6 servings

Turkey Chili & Cauliflower Rice

Total Time
80 minutes

Ingredients
1 lb. ground beef
1 lb. ground sausage
2 cups tomatoes, diced
1 yellow onion, diced
1 tsp. ground cumin
2 tbsp. chili powder
1/4 cup water
1 head cauliflower
2 fresh chili peppers
Olive oil

Directions
1) Cook beef and sausage in a skillet until browned then drain fat.
2) To a large pot add beef, sausage, onion, tomatoes, chili powder, cumin, and water. Stir well and cover.
3) Cook over medium heat for 1 hour.
4) Place the cauliflower in a food processor and pulse into rice sized grains.
5) In a large skillet, sauté the cauliflower in olive oil until tender.
6) Serve cauliflower rice topped with chili and fresh chopped chili peppers.

Yield
6 servings

Shrimp Alfredo

Total Time
20 minutes

Ingredients
3 cloves garlic, minced
1/2 cup parmesan cheese, grated
1 cup heavy cream
2 tbsp. butter
1 tsp. dried basil
1 lb. shrimp
Salt
Pepper

Directions
1) In a medium pan, add garlic and butter. Heat until mixture begins to simmer.
2) Add heavy cream and let simmer for 2 minutes.
3) Slowly add parmesan cheese and stir to mix.
4) Add basil and salt and pepper to taste.
5) Simmer for an additional 5 minutes.
6) Clean shrimp, ensuring shells, tails, and deveined.
7) Add shrimp to sauce mixture and simmer for an additional 5 minutes.
8) Add to top of zucchini noodles or low carb vegetable of your choice.

Yield
4 servings

Buffalo Chicken Meatballs

Total Time
40 minutes

Ingredients
1 lb. ground chicken
4 oz. cream cheese
1/4 cup parmesan cheese, grated
1 tsp. garlic powder
1/4 cup almond flour
1/4 cup blue cheese crumbles
4 slices bacon
1/3 cup buffalo sauce
Olive oil

Directions
1) Preheat oven to 350 °F.
2) In a large mixing bowl add ground chicken, almond flour, parmesan cheese, and garlic powder. Mix well.
3) Lightly coat a large baking pan with olive oil.
4) Evenly place golf ball sized meatballs in a baking pan and cover with aluminum foil.
5) Bake for 30 minutes.
6) In a small mixing bowl add cream cheese and blue cheese crumble. Mix well.
7) Cook bacon and chop into small pieces.
8) Spread cheese mixture on plate and top with meatballs. Add buffalo sauce to taste and top with chopped bacon.

Yield
4 servings

Broccoli Cheddar Soup

Total Time
35 minutes

Ingredients
3 cups broccoli, chopped
1 cup heavy cream
1 tsp. butter
3 cloves garlic, minced
2 1/2 cups vegetable broth
3 cups cheddar cheese, shredded
2 slices bacon
Salt
Ground black pepper

Directions
1) Melt butter in a saucepan over medium heat.
2) Add garlic and cook until tender.
3) Add vegetable broth, heavy cream, and broccoli.
4) Bring to boil. Simmer until broccoli is tender.
5) Add cheddar cheese gradually, stirring constantly, until completely melted.
6) Cook bacon and chop into small pieces.
7) Add chopped bacon pieces and stir to mix.
8) Season with salt and pepper to taste.

Yield
4 servings

Crispy Wings – Buffalo & Garlic Parmesan

Total Time
70 minutes

Ingredients
3 lb. chicken wings
1/2 tsp. baking soda
1/2 tsp. garlic powder
3 tsp. salt
1 1/2 tsp. ground black pepper
1 1/4 tsp. onion powder
1/2 cup buffalo sauce
4 tbsp. butter
2 tbsp. parmesan cheese, grated
1 tsp. garlic powder

Directions
1) Preheat oven to 250 °F.
2) Line a rimmed baking sheet with a double foil layer then set a wire baking rack over the foil.
3) In a large mixing bowl add baking soda, garlic powder, salt, pepper, and onion powder. Mix well.
4) If wings are frozen, thaw and pat dry with a paper towel.
5) Toss wings in spice mixture until evenly coated.
6) Arrange wings evenly on a baking rack.
7) Baking wings for 25 minutes.
8) Increase oven temperature to 450 °F and continue baking for 15 minutes.
9) Remove wings from oven and turn each over, then bake for another 15 minutes.
10) While wings are baking, melt butter and add grated parmesan cheese and garlic powder. Stir to mix.
11) Heat buffalo sauce in skillet or microwave.
12) Allow wings to cool for 5 minutes, then toss wings in your choice of sauce until evenly coated.

Yield
4 servings

Bacon Cheeseburger Soup

Total Time
60 minutes

Ingredients
1 lb. ground beef
6 slices bacon
3 tbsp. tomato paste
3 cups beef broth
1 cup cheddar cheese, shredded
4 oz. cream cheese
2 spears dill pickles, chopped
1 tbsp. steak sauce
2 tsp. spicy brown mustard
1 tsp. onion powder
1 tsp. chili powder
1 tsp. ground black pepper
1 cup romaine lettuce, chopped
1/2 cup grape tomatoes, halved
1/4 cup red onion, chopped

Directions
1) In a large skillet cook ground beef until brown.
2) Transfer beef to a large soup pot and add broth, cheddar cheese, cream cheese, pickles, tomato paste, steak sauce, mustard, onion powder, chili powder, and black pepper. Mix well.
3) Cook over medium heat until cheese is fully melted. Stirring continuously.
4) Reduce heat to low and cook soup for an additional 25 minutes.
5) Cook bacon and chop into small pieces.
6) Top bowls of soup with chopped bacon, lettuce, grape tomatoes, and red onions.

Yield
4 servings

Avocado Crab Boats

Total Time
20 minutes

Ingredients
5 medium ripe avocados
12 oz. lump crabmeat, drained
1/2 cup mayonnaise
2 tbsp. lemon juice
2 tbsp. fresh cilantro, chopped
1 chili pepper, minced and seeded
2 tbsp. chives, minced
1/4 tsp. ground black pepper
1 cup pepper jack cheese, shredded
1/2 tsp. paprika

Directions
1) Preheat oven broiler.
2) Wash avocados. Peel and cut into halves.
3) Place two avocado halves in a large bowl and mash lightly with a fork.
4) Add mayonnaise and lemon juice. Mix well until blended.
5) Stir in crab, cilantro, chives, chili pepper, and black pepper.
6) Spoon mixture into remaining avocado halves.
7) Line baking sheet with foil.
8) Transfer filled avocado halves to a baking sheet and top with shredded cheese and paprika.
9) Broil for 5 minutes.

Yield
8 servings

Sausage Cobb Salad Lettuce Wraps

Total Time
25 minutes

Ingredients
1 lb. ground sausage
6 large iceberg lettuce leaves
3/4 cup ranch salad dressing (low carb)
1/3 cup blue cheese crumbles
1 tbsp. fresh chives, minced
1 medium ripe avocado
4 large hard-boiled eggs
1 medium tomato, chopped

Directions
1) Cook ground sausage in large skillet and crumble into small pieces, drain, and stir in chives.
2) In a medium mixing bowl add ranch dressing, and blue cheese. Mix well.
3) Clean and dry lettuce leaves. Trim as needed.
4) Wash avocado. Peel and chop into bite-sized pieces.
5) Remove shells from hardboiled eggs and rinse with cool water. Chop into small pieces.
6) Spoon sausage onto lettuce leaves.
7) Top with avocado, eggs, and tomato.
8) Drizzle dressing mixture on top.

Yield
6 servings

Spicy Thai Coconut Chicken Soup

Total Time
60 minutes

Ingredients
1 lb. chicken breast
1 large onion, chopped
1 can light coconut milk
2 tbsp. coconut flour
3 tbsp. canola oil
1 small jalapeno pepper, seeded and minced
2 garlic cloves, minced
2 tsp. red curry powder
1 tsp. ground ginger
3/4 tsp. salt
1/2 tsp. ground turmeric
1 tsp. Sriracha chili sauce
32 oz. chicken broth
2 cups cabbage, thinly sliced
1 cup snow peas, thinly sliced
Green onions, thinly sliced
Lime wedges

Directions
1) Cut chicken into 1/2 inch cubes.
2) Toss chicken with coconut flour. In large stockpot, heat oil over medium-high heat. Sauté chicken until golden brown. Remove from pot.
3) In the same pot, sauté onion, jalapeno, and garlic over medium-high heat until onion is tender.
4) Add curry powder, Sriracha, coconut milk, and broth. Bring mixture to boil, then reduce heat and simmer for 20 minutes covered.
5) Stir in cabbage, snow peas, and chicken. Cook for an additional 5 minutes.
6) Serve with green onions and lime wedges.

Yield
6 servings

Crab Stuffed Mushrooms with Cream Cheese

Total Time
45 minutes

Ingredients
20 full baby portabella mushrooms
4 oz. lump crab meat, chopped
4 oz. softened cream cheese
5 cloves garlic, minced
2 tbsp. parmesan cheese, grated
1 tsp. dried oregano
1/2 tsp. paprika
1/2 tsp. ground black pepper
1/4 tsp. salt

Directions
1) Preheat oven to 400 °F.
2) Line a baking sheet with parchment paper.
3) Remove stems from mushrooms and discard.
4) Place mushroom caps on baking sheet and season with salt.
5) In a large mixing bowl add cream cheese, crab meat, garlic, oregano, paprika, black pepper, and salt. Mix well.
6) Stuff mushroom caps with mixture and sprinkle with parmesan cheese.
7) Bake for 30 minutes or until mushrooms are tender and tops are golden brown.

Yield
4 servings

Italian Hoagie Biscuits

Total Time
55 minutes

Ingredients
1 1/4 cup almond flour
1 cup deli meats, chopped
1 cup provolone cheese, shredded
4 oz. cream cheese
1 large egg
1/4 cup heavy cream
1/4 cup water
1 packet Italian dressing mix

Directions
1) Preheat oven to 350 °F.
2) In a blender add cream cheese, egg, water, heavy cream, and Italian dressing mix. Blend until smooth.
3) In a medium mixing bowl add almond flour and the mixture from blender. Mix well.
4) Stir in chopped deli meat and shredded cheese.
5) Place biscuit mixture into silicone muffin pan.
6) Bake for 20 minutes.

Yield
12 servings

Chicken Enchilada Casserole

Total Time
40 minutes

Ingredients
3 fresh jalapenos, chopped
1 fresh jalapeno, sliced
1/2 white onion, diced
1/2 cup heavy cream
4 oz. cream cheese
1 cup red enchilada sauce
1 lb. chicken breast, cooked, shredded
2 low carb flour tortillas
1 cup Mexican cheese blend, shredded
Olive oil

Directions
1) Preheat oven to 350 °F.
2) In a large skillet add a small amount of olive oil, chopped jalapenos, and diced onion. Sauté over medium heat until vegetables become soft.
3) Add to the skillet heavy cream and cream cheese. Stir until everything is well mixed and melted.
4) Add to the skillet enchilada sauce and shredded chicken. Mix well.
5) Slice tortillas into strips.
6) In a large baking dish lightly coated with olive oil, add half of the tortilla strips, followed by half the chicken enchilada mixture. Then add the remaining tortilla strips and remaining chicken enchilada mixture.
7) Cover the top with shredded cheese and sliced jalapenos.
8) Cover the baking dish with foil and bake for 15 minutes.
9) Remove foil cover and bake for an additional 15 minutes.

Yield
6 servings

Personal Pizza

Total Time
10 minutes

Ingredients
3/4 cup mozzarella cheese, shredded
1/2 cup tomato sauce (no sugar added, unseasoned)
1 tsp. oregano
1/2 tsp. garlic powder
1/2 tsp. red pepper flakes
4 slices pepperoni

Directions
1) Place 1/2 cup of shredded mozzarella cheese in a cool frying pan and cook over medium heat.
2) In a small bowl add tomato sauce, oregano, garlic powder, and pepper flakes. Mix well.
3) Once the cheese is melted and starting to turn brown, reduce heat and gently lift cheese from pan with a spatula to ensure it is not stuck.
4) Add tomato sauce mixture to the top of cheese crust and spread it to the edges.
5) Cover the tomato sauce with the remaining mozzarella cheese and top with pepperoni slices.
6) Wait until top cheese is melted, then allow to cool a couple minutes before eating.

Yield
1 serving

Chicken Quesadilla

Total Time
20 minutes

Ingredients
1 small chicken breast, cooked, shredded
1 low carb flour tortilla
1/2 avocado, sliced
1/4 cup pepper jack cheese, shredded
1 tsp. jalapeno, chopped
1/4 tsp. red pepper flakes
1/4 tsp. garlic powder
1/4 tsp. salt
Olive oil

Directions
1) Lightly coat frying pan with olive oil.
2) Lay tortilla flat in pan and heat over medium heat.
3) Once tortilla begins to get hot, cover tortilla with pepper jack cheese.
4) Add chicken, avocado, and jalapeno to one half of the tortilla.
5) Fold tortilla over and press down with a spatula.
6) Remove from heat once everything is melted together.

Yield
1 serving

Chicken Peanut Pad Thai

Total Time
30 minutes

Ingredients
2 chicken breast, cooked, shredded
2 large zucchini
1 white onion, chopped
1 egg
2 cloves garlic, minced
2 tbsp. soy sauce
1 lime
1/2 tsp. red pepper flakes
1 oz. roasted peanuts, shelled
Olive oil

Directions
1) Cut zucchini into noodles using spiralizer, set aside.
2) In a large pan add a small amount of olive oil, chopped onion, and garlic. Sauté over medium heat until onions become soft.
3) In the center of the pan add egg and allow the egg to cook slightly then scramble it into large pieces.
4) Add zucchini noodles and toss in egg and onion mixture. Cook noodles for approximately 3 minutes, tossing continuously.
5) Add chicken, soy sauce, lime juice, and red pepper flakes. Stir to mix.
6) Serve with crushed peanuts and a lime wedge.

Yield
4 servings

Buffalo Chicken Lettuce Wraps

Total Time
25 minutes

Ingredients
2 lbs. chicken breast
1 head butter lettuce
1/2 red bell pepper, diced
1/2 green bell pepper, diced
1/2 cup hot sauce
1/2 cup blue cheese crumbles
2 tbsp. butter
2 tsp. onion powder
1 tsp. garlic powder
2 scallions, chopped

Directions
1) In a large skillet add butter and diced peppers. Sauté over medium heat until vegetables become soft.
2) Cut chicken breasts into bite-sized pieces.
3) Add chicken, onion powder, and garlic powder to the skillet. Stir to mix until chicken is completely cooked.
4) Add hot sauce and sauté for an additional 3 minutes.
5) Remove skillet from heat and stir in blue cheese crumbles and chopped scallions.
6) Fill butter lettuce leaves with buffalo chicken mixture.

Yield
4 servings

Appetizers & Sides

Zucchini French Fries

Total Time
45 minutes

Ingredients
2 zucchini
2 eggs
3/4 cup parmesan cheese, grated
1 1/2 tsp. garlic powder
1 tsp. paprika
1/2 tsp. ground black pepper
Olive oil

Directions
1) Preheat oven to 425 °F.
2) Cut zucchini into 1/2 inch slices.
3) Line baking sheet with foil and lightly coat with olive oil.
4) In a large bowl, beat eggs.
5) In a second large bowl, combine parmesan cheese, garlic powder, paprika, and black pepper. Mix well.
6) Dip zucchini in beaten eggs, then dip in parmesan mixture until fully coated.
7) Place evenly spaced on a baking sheet.
8) Bake for 30 minutes or until golden and crispy.

Yield
4 servings

Cheesy Bacon Biscuits

Total Time
40 minutes

Ingredients
1 head cauliflower
2 eggs
1 clove garlic, minced
3/4 cup cheddar cheese, shredded
1 tbsp. coconut flour
4 slices bacon, chopped
2 tbsp. green onion, chopped
1/2 tsp. salt
1/8 tsp. ground black pepper
Olive oil

Directions
1) Preheat oven to 400 °F.
2) Place the cauliflower in a food processor and pulse into small rice sized grains.
3) In a large skillet, add cauliflower and garlic, sauté in olive oil until tender.
4) In a large bowl, beat eggs. Stir in coconut flour until dissolved.
5) Add cauliflower mixture, cheddar cheese, salt, pepper, and green onions. Mix well.
6) Lightly coat silicone muffin tins with olive oil and fill with mixture.
7) Bake for 25 minutes.

Yield
6 servings

Crispy Spicy Cauliflower Pancakes

Total Time
50 minutes

Ingredients
2 cups cauliflower, grated
2 tbsp. onion, chopped
1 clove garlic, minced
1 cup cottage cheese, drained
2 egg whites
2 tbsp. hot sauce
2 tsp. dried parsley
1 tsp. dried oregano
1/4 tsp. garlic powder
Olive oil

Directions
1) Preheat oven to 350 °F.
2) Line a baking sheet with parchment paper.
3) In a large skillet heat olive oil and add cauliflower, onion, and garlic.
4) Cook until soft, stirring to cook evenly.
5) Remove from heat and place in a bowl to cool.
6) In a blender add cottage cheese, egg whites, hot sauce, parsley, oregano, and garlic powder. Blend until smooth.
7) Add cheese mixture to cauliflower and mix evenly.
8) Spoon small pancakes onto a baking sheet.
9) Bake for 30 minutes, or until golden and crispy.
10) Add more hot sauce to taste.

Yield
4 servings

Cheesy Cauliflower Breadsticks

Total Time
50 minutes

Ingredients
6 cups cauliflower, grated
1 large egg
1/2 cup mozzarella cheese, shredded
1/2 cup parmesan cheese, grated
1/2 cup cheddar cheese, shredded
1/4 cup parsley, chopped
1/4 cup basil, chopped
1 clove garlic, minced
1 tsp. salt
1/2 tsp. ground black pepper

Directions
1) Preheat oven to 425 °F.
2) Line a baking sheet with parchment paper.
3) In a microwave safe bowl add cauliflower. Cover bowl and microwave on high until tender, about 10 minutes.
4) Allow cauliflower to cool until it can be handled, then wrap cauliflower in a clean kitchen towel and squeeze over the sink until dry. Return dry cauliflower to bowl.
5) In a large mixing bowl add mozzarella cheese, parmesan cheese, and cheddar cheese. Mix well.
6) Add half of the cheese mixture to the cauliflower. Mix well.
7) Add egg, basil, parsley, garlic, salt, and pepper to cauliflower. Mix well.
8) Spread cauliflower mixture onto baking sheet forming an even layer.
9) Bake for 25 minutes or until the edges are golden brown.
10) Top with remaining cheese mixture and bake for an additional 10 minutes.
11) Allow to cool for 5 minutes and cut into break stick shape.

Yield
8 servings

Sweet Onion Swiss Dip

Total Time
35 minutes

Ingredients
3 cups sweet onions, chopped
2 cups Swiss cheese, shredded
2 cups mayonnaise
2 tsp. hot sauce
1/4 cup horseradish
Ground black pepper
Olive oil

Directions
1) Preheat oven to 375 °F.
2) In a large mixing bowl add onions, shredded cheese, mayonnaise, horseradish, and hot sauce. Mix well.
3) Lightly coat a large baking dish with olive oil.
4) Transfer mixture to baking dish.
5) Bake for 25 minutes or until the edges are golden brown.
6) Sprinkle with ground black pepper.
7) Serve with your favorite low carb vegetable or chip.

Yield
10 servings

Bacon Blue Cheese Deviled Eggs

Total Time
20 minutes

Ingredients
8 large hard-boiled eggs
1/3 cup mayonnaise
1/4 cup sour cream
1/4 cup blue cheese crumbles
1 tbsp. Dijon mustard
1/2 tsp. salt
1/2 tsp. pepper
1/4 tsp. fresh dill, chopped
3 slices bacon
1 tbsp. parsley, chopped

Directions
1) Remove shells from hardboiled eggs and rinse with cool water.
2) Cut eggs in half lengthwise.
3) Remove yolks and place them in a medium mixing bowl. Keep egg whites to the side.
4) Cook bacon in a skillet. Chop cooked bacon into fine pieces.
5) With a large spoon mash egg yolks and add sour cream, mayonnaise, bacon, mustard, dill, salt, and black pepper.
6) Spoon mixture into egg whites and chill.
7) Top with chopped parsley.

Yield
3 servings

Bacon Wrapped Jalapeno Poppers

Total Time
35 minutes

Ingredients
16 fresh jalapenos
4 oz. cream cheese
16 slices bacon
1/4 cup cheddar cheese, shredded

Directions
1) Preheat oven to 350 °F.
2) Cut each piece of bacon in half.
3) Cut the end off of each jalapeno and cut in half length-wise. Remove seeds and inner core.
4) In a small bowl add cream cheese and cheddar cheese. Mix well.
5) Fill each jalapeno half with cheese mixture then wrap with bacon.
6) Line baking sheet with foil and lightly coat with olive oil.
7) Place bacon wrapped jalapeno popper on a baking sheet.
8) Bake for 25 minutes.

Yield
16 servings

Zucchini Nacho Chips

Total Time
20 minutes

Ingredients
1 large zucchini
1 oz. taco seasoning or ranch seasoning
Vegetable or coconut oil

Directions
1) Cut zucchini into thin discs using a mandolin.
2) In a large bowl toss zucchini chips with salt, allow chips to sit for 5 minutes, then dry.
3) In a frying pan add oil and heat to 350 °F.
4) Fry zucchini chips until they turn golden brown.
5) Remove from oil and lay on paper towel.
6) While still hot, sprinkle with taco or ranch seasoning, or both!

Yield
4 servings

Mediterranean Portabella Slices

Total Time
20 minutes

Ingredients
12 oz. portabella mushrooms
2 tbsp. olive oil
2 tbsp. balsamic vinegar
1/2 tsp. basil
1/2 tsp. thyme
1/2 tsp. rosemary
1/2 tsp. tarragon

Directions
1) In a medium bowl add olive oil, balsamic vinegar, rosemary, tarragon, basil, and thyme. Mix well.
2) Cut portabella mushrooms into 1-inch slices.
3) Brush oil mixture onto both sides of mushroom slices.
4) Cook mushrooms in a large skillet over medium-high heat. Flip halfway to cook both sides.

Yield
4 servings

Sweet & Spicy Brussels Sprouts

Total Time
20 minutes

Ingredients
1 lb. Brussels sprouts
2 tbsp. sesame seed oil
1 tbsp. Sriracha
1 tbsp. soy sauce
2 tbsp. brown sugar Erythritol sweetener
1/4 tsp. ground black pepper
1 tbsp. sesame seeds
1 tbsp. green onion, chopped

Directions
1) In a large bowl add sesame seed oil, soy sauce, Sriracha, brown sugar Erythritol, and black pepper. Mix well.
2) Trim Brussels sprouts and cut into quarters.
3) Cook Brussels sprouts in a large skillet over medium-high heat for 3 minutes. Flip Brussels sprouts and cook for an additional 3 minutes.
4) Pour sauce over Brussels sprouts and cook for an additional 2 minutes.
5) Sprinkle sesame seeds and green onions on top.

Yield
4 servings

Desserts

Peanut Butter Cookies

Total Time
20 minutes

Ingredients
1 cup peanut butter
1/2 cup powdered Erythritol sweetener
8 tbsp. butter
1 tbsp. coconut flour
1 tsp. vanilla extract
1/2 tbsp. ground cinnamon
1/2 tsp. salt

Directions
1) Preheat oven to 350 °F.
2) In a large mixing bowl add peanut butter, Erythritol, coconut flour, vanilla, cinnamon, and salt. Mix well until thick dough texture.
3) Melt butter and add melted butter to the dough mixture. Mix well.
4) Line cookie sheet with parchment paper.
5) Use a cookie scooper to place 12 dough balls on cookie sheet.
6) Bake for 15 minutes.

Yield
6 servings

Chocolate Cheesecake

Total Time
100 minutes

Ingredients
24 oz. cream cheese, softened
3/4 cup sour cream
3 eggs
5 tbsp. butter, softened
1 1/2 tsp. vanilla extract
2 tsp. cacao powder
1 cup powdered Erythritol sweetener

Directions
1) Preheat oven to 300 °F.
2) In a large bowl add softened cream cheese and butter.
3) Mix until smooth with electric mixer.
4) Add sour cream and mix well.
5) Add one egg at a time and mix well.
6) Add vanilla, cocoa powder, and powdered Erythritol. Mix well until smooth.
7) Place parchment paper in the bottom of a 9-inch springform pan. Pour cheesecake mixture into springform pan.
8) Place pan on a cookie sheet and bake for 90 minutes.
9) Allow cheesecake to fully cool. Then put in refrigerator overnight before serving.

Yield
8 servings

Minnie Blueberry Cheesecakes

Total Time
130 minutes

Ingredients
4 oz. cream cheese, softened
3/4 cup fresh blueberries
1/4 cup coconut oil
4 tbsp. unsalted butter
2 tbsp. powdered Erythritol sweetener
1 tbsp. lemon juice
1 lemon zest

Directions
1) In a large mixing bowl add cream cheese, butter, coconut oil, and Erythritol. Mix well until creamy.
2) Using a high-speed blender, blend the blueberries.
3) Add blueberries, lemon juice, and lemon zest to the cheese mixture. Mix well.
4) Place cheesecake mixture into silicone muffin pan.
5) Lightly press additional fresh blueberries into the top of cheesecakes.
6) Freeze for 2 hours.

Yield
8 servings

Double Chocolate Cake

Total Time
60 minutes

Ingredients
2 cups almond flour
2 tbsp. coconut flour
1 cup powdered Erythritol sweetener
1 1/2 baking soda
1/2 tsp. salt
1 cup butter
1/2 cup cocoa powder
1 cup water
3 eggs
2 tsp. vanilla extract
1/2 cup sour cream
3 tbsp. powdered Erythritol sweetener
1 tsp. vanilla extract
2 tbsp. heavy cream

Directions
1) Preheat oven to 350 °F.
2) In a large bowl whisk together almond flour, coconut flour, powdered Erythritol, baking soda, and salt.
3) In a small pot over medium heat add butter, cocoa powder, and water. Stir together until melted and well combined.
4) Pour half chocolate mixture into dry ingredients and stir to mix. Once the mixture is thick add the other half of chocolate mixture and mix well.
5) Add eggs one at a time.
6) Add sour cream and vanilla. Mix well.
7) Add batter to greased medium cake pan.
8) Bake for 40 minutes.
9) In a small bowl add heavy cream, powdered Erythritol, and vanilla extract. Mix well and chill in the refrigerator. Stir every 5 to 10 minutes.
10) Once the cake is finished baking and cooled. Pour glaze evenly over the top.

Yield
10 servings

Chewy Ginger Cookies

Total Time
25 minutes

Ingredients
1 1/2 cups almond flour
3/4 cup coconut flour
3/4 cup unsalted butter, softened
3/4 cup brown sugar Erythritol sweetener
1 egg
1/2 tbsp. ground ginger
1 tsp. ground cinnamon
1/4 tsp. salt

Directions
1) Preheat oven to 350 °F.
2) Line cookie sheet with parchment paper.
3) In a large bowl whisk together almond flour, coconut flour, ginger, cinnamon, and salt.
4) In a separate large bowl add butter and brown sugar Erythritol and beat until light and fluffy.
5) Add the egg to the butter mixture.
6) Slowly add try mixture. Mix well.
7) Once the dough is well mixed, use a cookie scooper to place 12 dough balls on cookie sheet.
8) Gently flatten each cookie then bake for 10 minutes.

Yield
12 servings

Printed in Great Britain
by Amazon